CREATIVE WRITING 101

Also by Stuart Albright

Blessed Returns
Sidelines
Bull City
A World Beyond Home

CREATIVE WRITING 101

Lessons from an Innovative Classroom

Stuart Albright

MCKINNON
PRESS
Durham, NC

MCKINNON PRESS
2704 Bexley Avenue
Durham, NC 27707
(919) 943-6501

Special discounts are available on bulk orders of this book. To inquire, please contact Stuart Albright at stuartalbright@yahoo.com.

Dedicated to the Writers of Room 413

Table of Contents

Chapter 1
Introduction

A Creative Writing Manifesto

Why do we write?

It's a simple question with a complex answer.

Why do we breathe? Why do we get out of bed in the morning?

I'm a rule follower, so I do what I'm told. I work hard so that I can make money and pay the bills, which keeps my family fed and off the streets. I believe that productivity usually leads to success and happiness – a spouse, a few kids, a reason to get out of bed in the morning, a life filled with purpose.

Maybe you write for fun. Maybe you write because books have opened your eyes and made you see the world in a whole new way.

I want to do that, you think. *I want to shine that light for other people.*

For me, writing is therapy. I sit down at the computer and let a complicated idea work its way through my brain – something that confuses me or makes me angry. I want clarity, and sometimes the only way I get that clarity is by placing my thoughts on paper.

For over a decade, I've guided my students through this process. I've taught over 1,500 teenagers from all walks of life. AP students, limited English learners, athletes, poets, gang members – you name the group and I've have taught them. It's been messy at times. I haven't reached everyone, and those *ah-hah* moments don't come as often as I'd like. Like most people, I want the Hollywood ending, the *Freedom Writers* classroom in which the teacher literally saves her student from themselves. But the real world doesn't work that way.

In spite of this, I still believe that creative writing is one of the most powerful art forms imaginable. From time to time I'll get an email or Facebook message from a former student – often the kid who made my life a living hell – asking if I remembered that one starter we did in class (*I've always loved the smell of rainfall and gasoline…*), or the time Jose stood on the table and we had to describe him, or the time when Jackie wrote for the first time about losing her father to gun violence.

Creative writing changed me, they say to me again and again.

And it can change you.

"When will I ever use this class in the real world?"

Every teacher must be prepared to answer this question. It often comes from the cynical student who doesn't want to do any work, but it can also come from a genuine place:

I'm here every day for eight hours, then I go home and do more school work until it's time to go to bed, and then I wake up to do it all over again. What the hell for?

I can't speak for math or science classes, but I'm happy to defend writing whenever the question comes up.

Why *do* stories matter?

Students aren't the only ones asking this question. Policy makers have sparked a national debate about literature's place in the curriculum. Should students be reading more "information texts" instead of novels? Are students spending too much time in imaginary worlds instead of learning how to read a text closely? I'll try to steer clear of this debate, but I can say without hesitation that stories matter.

C.S. Lewis addressed this topic eloquently when he wrote that stories give a reader "the dim sense of something beyond his reach and, far from dulling or emptying the actual world, give it a new dimension of depth. He does not despise real woods because he has read of enchanted woods: the reading makes all real woods a little enchanted. This is a special kind of longing."

Creative writing matters because all of us have a story to tell. Our lives are full of dreams and desires that may never come true, but that isn't the point. The dream is what gets us up in the morning. The dream shows us a world that we long to be a part of.

Fiction and reality blend together when a teenager writes a story (or in the case of my advanced writing class, a full-length novel.) An awkward kid like Ian gets to create a fantasy world with warlocks and other mystical creatures that go to battle against a brave warrior – the kind of noble hero that he hopes to be one day if he can just get through the loneliness of adolescence. His only friend in high school is Jeremy, who also writes fantasy stories. But Jeremy creates these worlds so that he doesn't have to think about his little sister as she battles cancer. He wants to be strong for her, like the noble knight. He will protect her against goblins and invisible armies with demonic eyes and deadly claws.

And then there's Alexus, who is writing a novel about teenage prostitutes living on the streets of New York. Alexus has a bit of a reputation around school. She has low self-esteem and admits to using sex as a way to get attention. She is not a prostitute, but this character allows her to explore what it feels like to be used, to be nothing more than an object. On the other side of the classroom is Rachel, a quiet girl whose grades have begun to slip in my class. I don't know what's happened to her until I read her story. It is about a lonely girl who tries marijuana for the first time because a cute boy asks her to. The boy makes her feel pretty, and the weed deadens the pain of being alone. Before long she can't tell truth from fiction. Does the boy love her, or is she merely an accessory to his drug addiction?

I've learned more than I ever need to know about teenage romance in my creative writing classes. I try to create a close, family atmosphere to encourage my students to write with an open heart. My students learn to respect each other. They also learn to see their classmates in a whole new light, and when you see someone in a whole new light you tend to form friendships that never would have happened otherwise.

You also tend to fall in love. I've lost count of the number of romances that have formed in my classes. When romance blossoms every year, writing gives me a unique window into the lives of my students. Roxanne was a white girl dating a black guy in my class, and she decided to explore this dynamic by writing a modern-day version of *Othello*, Shakespeare's groundbreaking play about an interracial couple. Three students in another class were involved in a convoluted love triangle that played out in each of their stories, with enough misunderstandings to make it clear to me that none of them really understood the true motivations of the other two.

More often than not, love was a weapon that did more harm than good. Linnie and Tay were in a passionate love affair that faltered as they each struggled with depression. One of them attempted suicide; the other wrote about it as a way to cope. Then the roles reversed when one of them started cutting. It was painful to read the ups and downs of their relationship over the course of the year. But it wasn't nearly as painful as the girl who wrote about her recent abortion – the hole that had formed in her heart, the guilt, the realization that her childhood had come to an end as soon as she left the clinic.

One of my best students was writing a novel about a saxophonist who was clearly modeled after himself; his main character had good grades, a beautiful girlfriend, and a very happy life. Midway through the school year my student stopped smiling when he came into my classroom. He was too kind to be rude to me, but something was clearly hurting him deep inside. I didn't have to wait long to find out. In his next submission, the novel took an unexpected turn when the main character's girlfriend died in a car accident. Turns out that my student's real-life girlfriend of three years had just dumped him for his best friend.

These stories could be exhausting to read. My brain could process hundreds of plotlines without overloading, but these weren't just stories. These were real people's lives – people who had entrusted me with their most vulnerable feelings. Every day I was absorbing the hopes, dreams, and fears of an entire generation of young people. They were standing at the edge of a precipice, waiting to jump into the great unknown. How could I not be inspired by such a leap of faith?

Learning through Trial and Error

I've read a lot of great writing from my students, but I've read plenty of bad writing as well. That's fine. We learn through our mistakes. We write really crappy first drafts and chip away at the fat until we've crafted something so clear and concise that people will look at our words and say, "Hey, that looks easy. I could do that." They rarely get a glimpse behind the curtain. They'll never know how many lines you crossed out or how many curse words you shouted because the damn thing wouldn't magically appear on the paper the way it sounded in your head.

Here are some of the common errors that I see in my novice writers:

1. Show, don't tell.

This one sounds simple enough, but very few writers walk the delicate line between *telling* us enough so that we're not confused and *showing* us the deeper truths of a story. Readers are our friends. We want to keep their attention, and we want them to feel as if they are discovering our story on their own. If a character is a jerk, the writer cannot simply say, "James Blumenthal was a jerk." But if James Blumenthal swipes $50 from the church collection plate and blows it on whiskey, the reader will come to that conclusion on her own. Now she's sucked into the story as an active participant.

The great minimalist Ernest Hemingway created the iceberg theory to deal with this dilemma. With an iceberg, we only see a tip of the ice above the ocean's surface, but underneath the iceberg is where the real danger lies. The trick is to decide how much of the ice we need to reveal. We want to hint at the complex world that our characters embody, and we want to bring our readers *into* this world, but we also don't want to overwhelm them. Time is a precious commodity. We want to lure our readers in without alienating them.

2. Use realistic dialogue.

It's easy to remember a conversation in our head. We can hear the nasal voice of our friend, the quirky slang, the rapid-fire pace of their words. But getting that conversation down on paper is a whole different story. We know right away when it doesn't ring true. *I can hear it in my head!* you scream as you stare at the inferior words on paper. Dialogue takes time and it takes practice.

3. Use the right amount of clear description.

When I start to read a new book, my head is an empty canvas. I want to read just enough clear and concise details to help me put color onto that canvas. At that point my imagination takes over, filling in the gaps and creating a vivid picture that's full of color and depth. The best writers give us a few specific details – a red wheel barrow glazed with rain water, the warm whoosh of stuffy air in a subway station – and then step out of the way so that we can take ownership of their story.

4. Write a strong opener that draws us in.

Over the years, I don't know how many times I've written the following words: "Try opening your story with a specific scene or image to draw us in." This doesn't mean that every story needs to begin with a knife fight or a sex scene. But it does mean that a reader should start painting their canvas as soon as a story begins.

5. Create well-rounded characters.

Our main characters usually share some semblance of our own personality. That's fine; we have to start with what we know. But the challenge comes when we have to look outside of ourselves to create characters that are nothing like us. This is particularly true with villains. I'm not a sexist, so how do I embody a character who *is* a sexist? I don't hate immigrants, so how do I write from the perspective of a bigot?

Empathy is a powerful skill in the writer's toolbox. It can make us uncomfortable at times, but it is necessary to create complex characters that feel real.

6. Find "truth" and originality in your own life.

How do you decide what will be interesting to your readers? Well, start with what you know. Be true to who you really are. Don't alter your style to fit a particular mold. Don't obsess about whether your writing is accessible to other people. The best art comes from the soul, not from some kind of formula for success.

7. You must have stamina.

It's hard to see a good idea through to the finish line. At the start, we're always bursting with excitement. *This is fun*, you think. Your big idea drives you forward with seemingly no end in sight.

Then you hit a wall. All of a sudden this whole writing thing feels like a chore. You could take a nap instead, or watch Netflix, or do just about anything else because the thrill is gone. Writing becomes work.

Here's where the dreamers separate themselves from the real writers. Writing is not fun all the time. In fact, it's not fun *most* of the time. But our best writing usually comes when we force ourselves to sit for that extra hour in front of the computer, slogging through a terrible draft and wondering if the right words will ever come to our fingertips again.

The journalist Walter Lippman once said that "Above all the other necessities of human nature, above the satisfaction of any other need, above hunger, love, pleasure, fame – even life itself – what a man most needs is the conviction that he is contained within the discipline of an ordered existence." Discipline and stamina are the bedrocks of creativity. Inspiration is great. Talent helps too. But the best writers have the willpower to sit there and keep writing even when the light goes out and we don't know if it will ever come back on again.

8. Avoid clichés at all cost.

It was all just a dream...
Just when Dana thought that her life was perfect, the oncoming truck barreled into her, killing her instantly...

We've seen these clichés a million times. Sure, they are convenient, and they can even be comforting because of their familiarity. But clichés do not inspire us. They do not make us want to keep reading. And while Mark Twain tells us that every possible story in the history of mankind has already been written, he goes on to say that all great art comes from the original twists that we make on our common conventions. So avoid clichés. They will put your reader to sleep or make her throw your story out the window.

9. Proofread your work carefully.

Read the following phrase quickly:

BOYS IN THE

THE HOOD

What did you see? Boys in the Hood? Or Boys in *the the* Hood?

I've used this activity in my classes for years, and even though this movie came out long before my students were born, they are familiar enough with the phrase to skip the second "the" almost every time. This happens because our brain is constantly unscrambling words on paper and reordering them in a way that makes sense. When you write a story and edit it again and again, your brain can no longer see the tiny errors that may be glaringly apparent to someone who has never read a draft of your story. So in addition to proofreading your work carefully, you need to get someone else to look at it with a fresh set of eyes. The only other option is to leave your story behind for a long enough period of time to de-program your brain from unscrambling the same phrases again and again.

Ignore this advice at your own peril. If you do, your final drafts may include embarrassing typos like the following:

One of my students wrote a powerful and deeply personal story about falling in love for the first time. He describes the girl by saying that he loved her "sweet, genital smile" instead of her *gentle* smile. And if that wasn't bad enough, he went on to describe their first kiss by saying "I was great" instead of "*It* was great." Funny, yes, but definitely not on purpose, and these two errors killed the intended mood of the story.

Now Write...

There are plenty of books out there about writing. Some of them are good; many of them are not. In fact, I only use a handful of books in my classroom. Instead, I have devised a creative writing curriculum that is battle tested by over 1,500 public school students. I've refined these lessons over the years, pulling ideas from hundreds of different sources. Some of my best activities have come directly from my students. *Why can't we do this...?* they'll ask me, and before I know it they are writing away happily; I'm just along for the ride.

I've structured this book the way that I structure my class. We'll start with a series of activities to get the ink flowing and prevent the dreaded writer's block before it begins. Then we'll move into the building blocks of writing such as point of view, dialogue, and description – the skills that all writers must master in order to get their points across clearly and concisely.

After that, I've included a serious of chapters on the different genres of writing. You will naturally gravitate to one form of writing more than another. But I've found over the years that understanding poetry has made me a better writer of prose, and that by picturing a story through the camera lens of a screenplay, I am more likely to create a plot that is visually appealing and well-paced. One genre blends into another, molding a writer into someone who cannot be confined in a box.

You may be interested in writing short stories, or a family memoir, or the next great American novel. Feel free to pick and choose the activities in this book that speak to you, and leave the rest behind. The writer Anne Lamott once said that "Life is like a recycling center, where all the concerns and dramas of humankind get recycled back and forth across the universe. But what you have to offer is your own sensibility."

There is no one like you in this world, and the way you synthesize another person's ideas will reflect that. Art builds on the beauty of centuries past, on conversations with our friends, on what we have suffered through.

My challenge to you is very simple: keep writing. These activities will give you the gentle nudge you need to find your own voice.

Our words have staying power. They remain when we have passed from this world.

What will your legacy be?

Chapter 2
Getting Started

I never liked the term "writer's block." Neither did Anne Lamott, whose book *Bird by Bird* is one of the few writing manuals I recommend to my students (the other one is *On Writing* by Stephen King – a clear, persuasive manual about the importance of simplification in writing.) So I'll borrow from Ann Lamott when it comes to "writer's block." I put these two words in quotations for a reason. Lamott argues that there is no such thing as writer's block; instead, you are merely empty.

This was a revelation for me as a writer. If you are blocked, there is a wall stopping your progress. The wall could be made out of concrete. It could be 20 feet tall, and thus you will never be able to get over it. As the doubt grows, so does the height of the wall.

So instead of being "blocked," what if we are merely empty? When our car is on "E," we simply fill it up. Humans are more complex than a vehicle, but there is a similar logic. If you are in a creative rut, you need to remove yourself from the situation. Take a walk in the woods, call a friend, laugh, live your life fully so that when you return to the keyboard, the doubts will have abated and you will be ready to get back to work.

Now just write. Let it all pour out, the good and the bad. Don't worry about being perfect. Just write and write and write and wait for the moment when the right words bubble to the surface, and they usually do if you just give it time.

One of the most common activities we do as a class involves starters. I provide the opening line of a story – something strange, or unexpected, or just plain off-the-wall. It really doesn't matter what I put on the board. The sentence is something to get the blood flowing over a finite period of time. We write for eight minutes, but you could go longer if you'd like. In fact, this opening sentence may be all you need to be off and running for the next two hours.

Here is a list of 80 starters that I have used in my classroom. There are a number of different variations to this activity, as you will see below:

1. Alice hated her mother…

2. I've always loved the smell of rainfall and gasoline…

3. "I love you, but…"

4. Some people say that _____ is the most beautiful word/phrase in the English language…

5. The bold writing on her t-shirt said it all: "_____"...

6. Loving/saving/killing her wasn't easy...

7. Pushing myself off the ground, I glared at her...

8. When I got home from the party, my parents were making out on the living room floor...

9. The headline in the Sunday newspaper read: "...

10. The sound of _____ seemed to come from everywhere...

11. Within my dreams, I saw...

12. I slipped, slid, and stumbled through...

13. He woke up to the taste of toothpaste and lipstick...

14. As I held him/her tight in my arms, I ...

15. I lost my...

16. As she picked up the phone, her eyes lit up. This was the moment she had been waiting for...

17. I slowly made my way up the stairs with a bra, a syringe, and a glass of orange juice...

18. Looking up at the sky, the rain pouring on my face, I realized…

19. This afternoon I ran into _____. Talk about an awkward moment…

20. Total silence, darkness everywhere, confusion on their faces, they continued to stare…

21. This is the second time this week I've been in _____…

22. As I walked into the airport, I heard someone scream, "Duck!"…

23. I heard a piercing scream, followed by blinding light…

24. As _____ walked into his/her first period class, everyone laughed and pointed…

25. If I could just get away…

26. I couldn't breathe. *What's happening?* I wondered…

27. As he held the _____ in his hand…

28. "I'm sorry, but I think this is the end for you,"…

29. Can you believe it? I was minding my own business when all of a sudden...

30. There I stood in the moment of truth, and it smashed into a million tiny pieces...

31. If _____ could have seen _____ earlier, things would be different...

32. Footsteps followed a dull sound at the bottom of the stairs...

33. I miss _____ when it rains...

34. Victoria walked into school that day with a purpose, and she wasn't leaving until the deed was done...

35. My whole life, I knew I was different...

36. He/she was perfect for me. Almost...

37. When the door opened, her date looked like a cross between _____ and _____...

38. The tattoo on her neck was in the shape of...

39. Caleb's deepest fear was finally a reality...

40. I threw the gun/drink/letter away...

41. I'd never been more ashamed in my life...

42. He/she woke up dazed, soaking wet, and tied to a chair...

43. I was 16 when I first met my older brother...

44. It only took one kiss/word/mistake/moment to screw everything up...

45. The detective raised his eyebrows when he entered the bloody classroom...

46. There it was, sitting on the kitchen counter...

47. He/she promised me forever...

48. Henry was the essence of rebellion, dressed in cargo shorts and combat boots...

49. When the radio started to play "_____," Crystal started to cry...

50. Guys never gave Maria much respect...

51. The girl sat in tears behind the dumpster...

52. He made me smile/want to throw up when he said those simple words: "_____"...

53. The city bus was always a _____ place for Jackie...

54. The cold knife was pressed against his/her throat...

55. No amount of pain/medication/money could keep Victor from ...

56. I woke up naked, covered in slugs...

57. He sat at the bar with a _____ in his back pocket...

58. When Frank got out of jail, the first thing he wanted to do was...

59. His/her eyes were like...

60. The letter in his hand said, "Meet me after school."...

61. He was in my first period class, and he didn't even care that I loved him...

62. The countdown began. "5, 4, 3, 2, 1"...

63. For the first time, Damian realized what hell was really like...

64. Kristen wanted him so bad that she was capable of...

65. The judge read the verdict to the courtroom: "Guilty/Not Guilty."…

66. It was the perfect plan…

67. Sarah woke up and felt her newly shaved head…

68. The color _____ always reminds me of…

69. Some people think it's weird that my parents are…

70. It's been one month, two days, and three hours since…

71. It was 2:00a.m., and I found myself in the middle of the city…

72. As the candle/house/car burned, she slowly…

73. There I stood in the moment of truth, and it smashed into a million tiny pieces…

74. In 2008, I was arrested for wounding a man in a movie theater…

75. My life was full of strange stories, some filled with beauty, others full of …

76. He ducked as a can of tomato juice was hurled at his head…

77. She was a backstabbing hypocrite, and she loved it…

78. In all my years, I never thought I would…

79. I hate you sometimes, but I need you… (personify some object/idea – Money, love, depression, makeup, cigarettes, etc.)

80. Life isn't easy when you're an ink pen…

Starter Variations

Instead of opening sentences, you can also use pictures, movie clips, or music to get started. Here are a few good resources:

1. Humans of New York – I love this photo blog by Brandon Stanton, who goes around taking pictures of everyday people in New York, often accompanied by short interviews (my favorite picture is of a tall, disheveled man leaning against a wall in Grand Central Station with a skateboard in hand. His explanation for being there: "I told her that if she wanted to start over, to meet where we first kissed. She was supposed to be here 15 minutes ago.")

2. "Walk Don't Walk" plaster sculpture by George Segal. I like to accompany this picture with the starter, "I stood on the corner, watching and waiting…"

3. "American Girl in Italy" photo by Ruth Orkin. In this classic black and white picture, a woman walks through a busy Italian street with men gawking at her. Try to write from the point of view of one of the people in this photo.

4. Google images are a great resource. I once found a picture of a solemn, mysterious girl staring out of a city window at night. Another time I found a picture of Ronald McDonald getting arrested by two cops.

5. Ripped from the headlines. Newspaper articles often provide great ideas for stories. In fact, I know of a handful of famous writers who get most of their ideas this way. In my hometown newspaper last year I found the following article: A man was arrested in a Walmart for allegedly sucking a woman's toe. In a much more serious article, an 11 year old boy was handcuffed to his front porch with a dead chicken hanging from his neck. Both of these articles immediately had my head spinning with story ideas.

6. College application essay prompts. Most college essay prompts are maddeningly boring, but UNC Chapel Hill used the following starters for an essay topic a few years back:

- It was a dark and stormy night...

- I heard a loud scream outside my window...

- What can you say when the world around you seems to be dying?...

- The landscape was brown and dry, devoid of any redeeming features...

- As I turned the corner, I saw the person who saved my life ten years ago...
- The last time I was in...

7. And then there are the opening lines of bestselling novels. You can find all kinds of these lists on the internet. Below are a few of my favorite openings:

- It was a wrong # that started it... (*The New York Trilogy* by Paul Auster)

- I am a sick man... (*Notes from the Underground* by Fyodor Dostoevsky)

- They shoot the white girl first... (*Paradise* by Toni Morrison)

- Elmer Gantry was drunk... (*Elmer Gantry* by Sinclair Lewis)

- It was the day my grandmother exploded... (*The Crow Road* by Ian Banks)

- I write this sitting in the kitchen sink... (*I Capture the Castle* by Dodie Smith)

- When Dick Gibson was a little boy, he was not Dick Gibson... (*The Dick Gibson Show* by Stanley Elkin)

- It was a pleasure to burn... (*Fahrenheit 451* by Ray Bradbury)

8. If you're looking for a little more fun, go with a classic "mad libs" starter:

1. write down any –ing verb (*thinking*, for example)
2. then write down a body part (*finger*)
3. then write down an inanimate object (*clock*)

Complete the following sentence by including each of the three words you came up with and keep writing:

After a long day of (<u>1</u>), he/she discovered that his/her (<u>2</u>) had turned into a (<u>3</u>)…

Chapter 3
The Building Blocks of Prose

In order to be an effective writer, we must first understand the basic building blocks of prose: point of view, description, character development, dialogue, and plot. Once we have mastered these concepts, we can dive into any genre of writing, whether it is short stories, poetry, or plays.

Point of View

Activity #1: Depth and Point of View

Read each of the following sentences as if they were different versions of the same opening line (adapted from John Gardner, *The Art of Fiction*):

Version #1: It was the winter of 1853. A large man stepped out of a doorway.

Version #2: Henry J. Washburn had never much cared for snowstorms.

Version #3: Henry hated snowstorms.

Version #4: God, how he hated those damn snowstorms.

Imagine yourself as a camera hovering high above a snowy night. In each of the four openers, the camera moves closer and closer to the subject, our good friend Henry. By the fourth version, we are literally *inside* his brain, learning his deepest thoughts. Each of these four versions conveys a very different point of view, even though the basic action stays the same. Our job as the writer is to choose the most appropriate point of view for the story we are trying to tell.

Activity #2: Zooming

1. Imagine a toll booth operator, 21 years of age, who works on the George Washington Bridge in New York.

2. Do a googlemaps search of the GW Bridge and zoom out to a point several hundred feet above the bridge, so that the cars on the bridge look like tiny toys.

3. Describe what you see (either literally or in your head) at four different points as you zoom down to this toll booth operator. By the final step, you should literally be in her head. What does she look like? What kind of personality does she have? How would our knowledge of these details affect the story we are about to write?

Activity #3: An Event in Multiple Points of View

Pick an unusual event that could happen in a confined space (for my students, I suggest a robbery, a girl going into labor, an alien invasion, etc.) Now write about this event from at least four different points of view, either in first person or in third person.

Activity #4: Argumentation

Choose a controversial topic that you have strong feelings about. Possible topics could be abortion, gun control, death penalty, drinking age, marijuana legalization, American troops overseas, sex education in public schools, the role of government in our daily lives, sports team allegiances, euthanasia, immigration, prayer in school, gay marriage.

Write this topic at the top of your paper. Now spend the next 10-15 minutes writing a passionate argument from the *opposite* side of this issue. My students hate when I say this. They groan. They shift uncomfortably in their desks. They complain that this is an impossible task. But then I pose a challenge to them: "If you can't put yourself in the shoes of someone you oppose, then you don't really know what you believe." This usually shuts them up.

Writers have to be able to show empathy – even towards the people we disagree with. As I mentioned earlier, we have to be able to write about characters that are not like us; otherwise we won't have a complex, multi-layered story.

Description

Activity #1: Careful Observation – The Detective

1. Choose a specific place (a classroom, a bedroom, the woods behind your house), and list every physical detail that stands out to you. Try to avoid the obvious and generic.

2. Get a friend or classmate to stand in front of you and do the same thing, describing everything you observe about this person, their facial features, what they are wearing, etc.

3. Take these two descriptive lists and circle the three most vivid details from each list. In a story, we can only include a finite number of details. Otherwise we will lose the reader's attention.

Activity #2: The Gritty Setting

1. Choose a place to describe that is gritty or repulsive. I like to go with a public school bathroom because – let's be honest – there is nothing more repulsive than a public school bathroom. Gas station bathrooms are a close second. You could also choose a back alley, the back seat of your car, or any number of places.

2. Write down every specific detail you see in this space – the grittier the better. If there is graffiti, don't just say that it is graffiti. Write down the exact words.

3. Now write a scene in which a character enters this repulsive place. Make this character as unfamiliar with this place as possible. What do they see? What do they feel?

What is going through their head? Be specific. I like to ask my students to write from the perspective of a wide-eyed freshman, formerly home-schooled, who is entering a public school restroom for the first time.

Activity #3: The Importance of Sound

1. As an introduction to sensory details in descriptive writing, play the first five minutes of a movie with the screen covered up. Make sure it is a movie that you haven't seen before. Now write down everything you "see" in your head. I often use the classic 80s movie *The Goonies* because it introduces a lot of interesting and varying sounds in the first five minutes.

2. Now play the scene again with the screen uncovered. Compare what you saw in your head with what was actually on the screen. There will typically be a lot of differences. This will give you a good idea about the importance of sensory details working together to form a unified picture in a story.

3. Take this activity a step further by choosing a setting that involves a lot of sounds. Examples could include a ball game, concert, jail, woods at night, earthquake, emergency room/hospital, school hallway, mall, airport, city bus, or haunted house. Now list as many specific sound details as you can think of for this kind of setting. Once again, avoid the banal or cliché. After you have completed this list, imagine a character that would be out of place in a setting

like this (an elderly woman at a heavy metal concert, for example.) Write a scene in which the sound details contribute to your character's discomfort in this unfamiliar setting.

Activity #4: The 5 Senses

1. Writes 5 senses on the board that trigger memories from your past. If you're really ambitious, try to write 5 examples for each of the 5 senses. For example:

> Smell of bacon
> Taste of sweet tea
> Sound of a subway train
> Feel of leather pigskin
> Sight of autumn leaves

2. Choose one of these sensory details and write for ten minutes about every memory you can associate with this particular sense.

Activity #5: 5 Senses, 5 Seconds

1. Choose a moment of great intensity in which the bulk of the action takes place in five seconds or less. It can be a euphoric moment, a moment of great shame, anything really (examples: a first kiss, a car crash, an injury, a fight, a break-up, getting caught in some kind of compromising position.)

2. Write a scene about this intense moment, using all five senses to describe this scene in vivid detail. This activity will

force you to focus on a tiny moment and expand the visual possibilities. Writers often make the mistake of glossing over these kinds of possibilities.

Activity #6: Going from flat to multi-layered using all five senses

1. Chose a photograph that that is either large in scope or involves a large number of people. I use a beautiful black and white photo of Grand Central Station in 1929, with sunlight streaming through the windows like spotlights.

2. Go through each of the five senses, and list as many details as possible to describe this setting.

3. Add 1-2 characters into this scene and write for 10 minutes. Who are these characters? Where are they going? What are they thinking about? When you are done, you will have taken a two dimensional picture and given it three dimensional depth.

4. If you want to take this activity a step further, go to a real place instead of looking at a picture and create a scene using all five senses. Really try to bring this scene to life, transforming a place that could otherwise feel flat and uninteresting to the common eye.

Character Development

Activity #1: Introduction to Character

1. Make a list of the kinds of qualities that make a person interesting (good or bad). From this list, circle the qualities that would most likely create an interesting character in a novel.

2. Write a descriptive paragraph about someone you know well. Describe not only the way that they look but also their personality. If you want to push yourself, try to do this activity with someone you *don't* know well. It will force your imagination to fill in the gaps of what you don't know.

3. Now imagine an ideal foil or villain for the person you described. If you were to set these two characters in a story, what would happen? Create a setting/conflict and write for at least 20 minutes.

Activity #2: Creating characters from their "stuff"

1. Choose a container from the following list: purse, wallet, gym bag, glove compartment, refrigerator, food pantry, desk drawer, school locker, briefcase, safety deposit box, car trunk, center consul, pockets, suitcase, book bag.

2. Create a character name, then list 10-15 specific items that could be found in this character's container.

3. This activity can be done individually, but it works best with a partner. Take your partner's list and imagine what their character is like based solely on the items in their

container. Give them an age, profession, physical description, and personality description.

4. For round 2, choose a character name, setting, and container. Switch this with your partner and have them come up with a list of items for your container. Once this is done, switch it back and try to flesh out your character's personality based on the items placed in your character's container. Now try to write an opening scene. The items in the container do not have to appear in the scene. They merely help us to create a full and interesting character.

Activity #3: Developed characters lead to new plot possibilities

1. Come up with a character name and answer the following prompts about them:
(Character list adapted from *Now Write* by Sherry Ellis)
- attitude of this character toward authority figures like their parents, boss, etc.
- perfect boyfriend/girlfriend
- most embarrassing or shameful moment in their past
- job they want vs. their actual job
- earliest memory of childhood happiness
- best memory of a romantic experience from their past
- describe their bed
- items in his/her refrigerator
- nervous behaviors/mannerisms
- biggest rival or enemy
- favorite place to relax

- person from the past s/he avoids at all costs
- biggest physical weakness
- biggest mental weakness

2. Like the previous exercise, this activity works best with a partner, but you can certainly do it individually as well. Switch your answers with a partner and create a scene with this new character. Describe what this character looks like, their personality, their day to day life, etc.

3. For Round 2, come up with a new character using the question prompts. Switch your character sheet with someone else, and try to create a story in which your character and your partner's character are combined into the same plot. Are they friends? Rivals? Lovers? See what kind of possibilities can be created when two very different characters are placed into the same story.

Activity #4: Internal vs. External Persona

1. This activity works best in a classroom setting. Take a blank sheet of paper and place a number at the top of each side (#1-999.) On one side of the paper, list words and pictures that describe how you think others see you (external.)

2. On the other side of the paper, list words and phrases that describe who you really are (internal.)

3. Collect the sheets, then place them on a random desk. Now go around the room with a new sheet of blank paper, jot down the number for each of the papers you look at, then jot down the one difference from internal/external that is most striking to you and try to guess who it is.

4. Once you have looked at every paper around the room and written down your responses, the teacher will reveal the names that go with each number so you can see how many you got right.

5. A teacher or student volunteer will now list some of the contrasts on the board between internal and external persona. Once this is done, choose the contrast that would work best for an interesting character in a story. Now try to create a character sketch in bullet point.

6. After this is done, write a scene in which your character's internal persona is revealed against their will.

Dialogue

Activity #1: Using dialogue subtly to tell a story

1. Before you do this activity, read Ernest Hemingway's classic short story, "Hills Like White Elephants." Hemingway does a great job of creating a tense scene between two people, even though the people never directly state the source of their tension.

2. After reading this story, write a 2-3 page scene that follows the same structure as Hemingway's story. Put two people into a scene that consists almost entirely of dialogue with little to no description after the opening paragraph. There must be some kind of tension between the two people, but the reader has to guess what that tension is without the characters directly mentioning the source of the tension. (spoiler alert: the couple in Hemingway's story are talking about getting an abortion. Other scenarios could include two men standing over a dead body without explicitly saying that they just killed this person; a married couple talking about getting a divorce without using the word "divorce"; a boy awkwardly asking a girl out on a date without using the word "date"; the possibilities are endless here. One effective way to trip up the reader is to send them down a wrong path intentionally.)

3. After you complete your scene, give it to someone to read and see if they can identify the unspoken source of the tension.

Activity #2: The Debate

1. Choose a controversial subject and debate a friend on this subject for 5-10 minutes.

2. After the debate, write down the key points that each side brought to the argument.

3. Now place two characters in a scene where this debate is the foundation of their dialogue.

Plot

Activity #1: Smashing Seed Ideas Together

1. Use the following four seed ideas as the starting point for a conflict:
- An old man sits, rocking and talking to himself on the subway.
- A little boy sees someone stealing money from the church collection plate.
- A woman on a cell phone says, "It's over, done with. I'm leaving tonight."
- A little girl walks through Manhattan alone, carrying a teddy bear.

2. Take your favorite seed idea from this list and brainstorm a story idea for at least 30 minutes.

3. Now take two of these seed ideas and smash them together into the plot of a new story. Brainstorm your story ideas for another 30 minutes. You will find that by combining two seemingly unconnected seed ideas, you can create a new and vibrant story idea.

4. You can also come up with your own seed ideas or get suggestions from a friend. Try to approach this with an open mind. At first you may not see how these two disconnected

ideas can be combined into a story, but that's kind of the point; when we open our minds to unexpected possibilities, we often create new and vibrant plot lines that never would have come to us otherwise.

Chapter 4
Poetry

Like politics, people have strong opinions about poetry; they either love it or they hate it. And even those who love poetry usually fall into the opposing camps of structured versus unstructured poetry.

Some of you (the poetry haters) may feel compelled to skip this chapter entirely. But don't despair! What I've found is that even my most vocal poetry critics leave this unit with a better appreciation for poetry.

Let's start with structured poetry and then move into unstructured poetry. There are countless ways to write poetry, just as there are countless ways to assess art. What does good poetry look like? Is it even possible to objectively state what a *good* poem looks like? In my classroom we approach this question indirectly. I place a hastily scribbled line on my front board and ask my students if this line qualifies as art.

Yes, some will say, *the squiggly line is art because you made the effort to place it on the board.*

Others will respond that it's not art because it was hastily drawn on the board. *How can it be art with so little thought?*

But how do we know there was little thought put into it? I like the line. It speaks to me, therefore it is art.

It doesn't speak to me, therefore it's not art.

The argument goes like this for a while before I put an end to the shouting and bring them back to the subject of poetry. There *are* underlying ways that we can measure a poem's effectiveness, but the way we approach poetry *is* rather subjective. Poetry is just one of many forms of expression. If you can say something in a concise way that moves another reader or creates a vivid picture in their head, you have accomplished one of the fundamental goals of any piece of writing. So whether you like poetry or hate it, there is value here.

Structured Poetry

The Haiku – The haiku is merely a three line poem that follows the set rhythm of 5 syllables on the first line, 7 syllables on the second line, and 5 syllables on the last line. Haikus are great because they can be done quickly while still giving the writer a genuine sense of accomplishment. And while they traditionally focus on nature, they certainly do not have to.

1. Start easy by filling in the middle line of the following haiku:

Green trees in the woods

_____ (7 syllables)

Standing tall and proud

2. Now take the following opening line and complete the haiku:

High school's narrow halls

_____ (7 syllables)

_____ (5 syllables)

3. Now try to write a haiku about your favorite aspect of nature. Then write one about someone you care about. Even the most reluctant poets usually dive headlong at this point. The whole point of the haiku is to make your point clearly and succinctly.

The Acrostic Poem – The acrostic poem is another form of simple but effective poetry. Take any word and list the letters down the left side of your paper. Now write a poem about this word using each letter to begin your lines of poetry.

A close cousin to the acrostic poem is the alphabet poem, in which every line begins with the next letter of the alphabet. If you like a challenge, this poem is for you (particularly as you get to the end of the alphabet and have to work with the letters X and Z.)

The Six Word Memoir – If you liked the challenge of the haiku, you will love the six word memoir. The concept is very simple: tell your whole life story in six words, no more, no less. The six word memoir got its start when a friend challenged Ernest Hemingway to write a story in six words (his response: "For sale: baby shoes, never worn.) Recently, *Smith Magazine* has held a six word memoir contest, with winners ranging from the deeply moving to the hilarious. Here are a few of my favorite winning entries:

Spent life waiting. Nothing ever happened.
Cursed with cancer, blessed with friends.
I still make coffee for two.
I like big butts, can't lie.
I never knew what hit me.
"Save me!" she begged. I couldn't.
He seemed so sweet. At first.
Married to ex-wife 150 pounds ago.

Now it's your turn. See if you can condense your entire life story into six words.

7X7X7 Poem – Like the seed ideas activity from the previous chapter, the 7x7x7 Poem will help you to find ideas in unexpected places.

1. Open a random book and turn to page 7.

2. Write down the 7th sentence on this page as the first line of your poem.

3. Write a 7 line poem using this opening line. You may have to do this activity several times before you find a sentence that really strikes a chord with your creativity. You

can also do any variation of the numbers – 5X5X5, for example, or 9X9X9.

Newspaper Blackout – This kind of poem is a new and rapidly growing art form. Take a newspaper article or any block of text. With a black marker, cross out all but a small number of words that, when combined, create entirely new phrases that are often deeply profound (check out www.newspaperblackout.com for some examples.)

Unstructured Poetry

Intro to Free Verse – I always start with this word activity, which allows my students to see their thoughts on paper in an unstructured form. Once they have done this, they can start making connections between the scattered words. It's a great visual representation of what goes through our minds when we create any kind of art from a jumble of unformed thoughts.

1. Take a sheet of paper and draw horizontal lines to divide the paper into three segments.

2. I give them a familiar word and ask them to write that word in the middle of the first segment and circle it (I usually start with "Jordan," the name of our high school.)

3. Over the next two minutes, write down every word or phrase that comes to mind when you think of the word "Jordan" (or whatever word you chose.) Most of the class

will think about things related to school, but then others will think about Michael Jordan, or Jordan Lake, or the country of Jordan. The responses are usually all over the place.

4. Do this activity again until you have filled up both sides of the paper. In the next third of the page, I'll give them the word "college," then "love" for the final segment. On the back side of the page, I ask them to choose a color, then a famous person, then an emotion other than hate.

5. At this point I ask my students to compare their list with someone next to them to see how many similarities and differences they can find.

6. Now take any one of these topics and weave a free verse poem out of the scattered words surrounding that topic.

Memory Poem

1. Create a chart with a horizontal line, starting with your birth and ending with the present.

2. On this horizontal line, plot out the following events: your earliest memory, your favorite memory, and finally your worst memory.

3. Now write a poem using one of these three memories. To make it more challenging, try adding one of the following variables:
  - water or other liquid or food

- mention a piece of furniture or object (bed, car, TV, etc.)

- include a sound, smell, or taste

- you can include one lie

Desire Poem – Write a poem about something you desire. It can be tangible, like sleep, or intangible, like racial justice. We all crave certain things, and these cravings can be great source material for your poetry.

Personification Poem – Write a personification poem in which the topic is a human character. Personified topics can include Money, Love, Sex, Happiness, Faith, Anger, Jealousy, Racism, Poverty, etc.

Simile/Metaphor Poem – Take something very basic that you do on a regular basis (like sleeping, or brushing your teeth, or falling in love) and create a poem using comparisons. Start with similes in the first two lines and then move to a mixture of similes and metaphors, allowing the rhythm of the comparisons to determine whether the word "like" is necessary at the beginning of each line.

Experiential Free Verse – Go outdoors to a place that is either very quiet or very loud. Allow the setting to influence the thoughts that come into your head. The serenity of the woods may open up your mind in refreshing ways. The busyness of a downtown street can open your mind in different ways, allowing unexpected thoughts and ideas to work into your brain. However you approach this, the important thing is to let your mind work as a sponge. Take everything in. Let it sit there and simmer for a bit. Then write.

Slam Poetry – In 1986, a poet and construction worker named Marc Smith approached the owner of the Green Mill, a Chicago jazz club that used to be Al Capone's favorite hangout. Smith wanted to start a Sunday night poetry competition that would be unlike anything the poetry world had seen before. Judges would score poems on a scale of one to ten. Poems would be performed more than read, with style counting almost as much as the content of the poem.

Marc Smith got his wish, and over the past three decades this competitive style of poetry has spread around the world.

Slam Poetry grew out of the Beat Generation, with poets like Allen Ginsberg breaking the conventions of rhythm and rhyme that had defined poetry for centuries. But the Beat Poets typically performed in mellow cafés, with audiences listening quietly, smoking cigarettes and nodding along to the poets on stage as they read in a monotone voice. Slam Poetry was a whole new ball game. Poets screamed and paced around the stage. They relied on audiences to snap their fingers and shout in response, harnessing enough energy to force the judges to give them the best possible score. Performance poetry was a contact sport, with style rivaling substance and the emotional response of the crowd determining a poem's success.

In the coming years a whole new art form came into being. Slam poetry took the wordplay of hip hop and combined it with storytelling and social activism. At its core, slam poetry was still poetry, but it made poetry relevant to people who felt marginalized and left out – blue collar guys like Marc Smith who still wanted to understand the world in all of its beauty, or young people who struggled to *see* the world that these poems invoked.

To write a slam poem, you can incorporate any of the poetry concepts I've listed above. Slam poems tend to be intense, delving deeply into social issues or personal experiences. They can make you laugh or cry. They will move you. And while the quality of writing plays a major factor, so too does the confidence with which these poems are performed.

Here are some specific activities that work well with slam poetry:

Activity #1 – Drawing on life experiences

1. Write your name and birthday at the top of your paper. Then list 20 things that have shaped who you are today. These can be people, events (good or bad), songs, books, etc. Try to list them in chronological order.

2. Write a 20 line poem addressed in the form of a letter to one of these persons or topics, explaining how this topic has shaped who you are today. The poem can rhyme or be free verse; it's up to you.

Activity #2: Breaking Stereotypes

1. On a note card, write down the following phrase and complete the blanks:

Don't think that just b/c I'm/I ___ means that I'm/I ___ .

Choose a stereotype that you've had to fight against at different points in your life. It could be related to your age, gender, race, friends, anything really (Examples: *Don't think that just because I'm a girl means that I can't be the head of the household,* or *Don't think that just because I'm a teenager means that I don't care about the world around me.*)

2. Now write a poem in which you take apart this stereotype.

3. Another approach is to get some friends to do this activity with you. Have them fill out their own note cards anonymously, switch them around, then try to write a slam piece using one of their stereotypes – even if it's not the kind of stereotype that you personally have to deal with. This can teach you empathy, which is one of the most important qualities for any good writer.

Activity #3: Alliteration Poem

Write a 20-30 line poem in which a specific sound repeats itself throughout the poem. Try to use a consonant like "B" or "T" instead of a vowel. Alliteration is an effective technique in slam poems, and while slam pieces use alliteration sparingly, writing an entire poem using this style will help you to see the musical quality of poetry (it's no coincidence that hip hop enthusiast often gravitate to slam poetry; plus, song lyrics are often nothing more than poetry put to music)

Rules of slam poetry: If you've never participated in a poetry slam, you should be aware of the following rules:

1. Poets cannot use any props when they perform their poem, other than their body.

2. Poems often have a time limit of two or three minutes. Any seconds over this time limit will deduct from the poem's final score.

3. In a poetry slam, five judges are usually chosen at random from the audience. The judges will score poems on a scale of one to ten, with one being the lowest and ten being the highest. The highest and lowest scores are then dropped, leaving the three middle scores (thus, the highest score a poet can receive is a 30.)

4. Slam poetry is also a collaborative art form. Group slam pieces can be incredibly powerful, and you often see these in the final rounds of a poetry slam.

To get a sense of what slam poetry looks like, you can find many examples online. Check out G Yamazawa on youtube, for starters. G is a former student of mine who was completely transformed by poetry in high school. Before that he was a drug dealer and a general troublemaker. Today he is one of the top slam poets in the country. There are also a number of excellent films about slam poetry. Among them are the documentaries *Slam Nation*, about the adult slam poetry scene; *Louder than a Bomb* and the HBO series *Brave New Voices*, which are both about the youth slam poetry scene; and *Slam*, a movie starring the legendary poet Saul Williams.

Chapter 5
Playwriting

Many writers struggle to use dialogue correctly in their stories. They use too much or too little. Their characters curse when they shouldn't curse (or vice versa), and they speak in formal English when they should use slang instead. Striking this balance can be difficult, but natural dialogue is vitally important if we want our stories to feel real.

Playwriting forces a writer to structure his/her plot around dialogue. Sure, you can use stage directions and other narrative devices to fill in the gaps, but dialogue is the driving force behind this genre.

Activity #1: The Monologue

Monologues often appear in the climactic scene of a play. Our main character gets to speak her piece, uninterrupted, to another character or directly to the audience (such as the Shakespearean soliloquy.) A secret is revealed, a character unloads a torrent of bottled up emotions – basically, this is the kind of scene that actors love because it is tailor-made for an Oscar or Emmy.

1. Look online at monologue examples from movies or plays, particularly storylines that you are familiar with. Then ask yourself the following question: what do we learn from these characters through their monologues? How does the narrative arc of this story change from this point forward?

2. Now let's practice by choosing a celebrity who is near and dear to our hearts. Write a monologue from that celebrity's point of view, having them speak to the audience or to another person (you, perhaps?) Possible emotions could include anger, lust, nervousness/paranoia, insanity, or narcissism.

Activity #2: Argument Scene

Write a 2-3 page scene using one of the following character combinations. Have them argue over a specific issue, with little to no character exposition or other stage directions.

If you want to challenge yourself, try to limit your use of profanity in this argument scene. I am no prude when it comes to coarse language, but I often find that writers will drop f-bombs into an argument simply because they can't think of anything else to write about. If you absolutely *have* to use profanity in your argument, try to limit it to one carefully placed expletive (which, you will likely discover, gives the curse word added power because it is withheld and then dropped like an unexpected bomb on your story.)

Character combinations to choose from:

parent/child
teacher/student
boyfriend/girlfriend
principal/student
parent/teacher
siblings
boss/employee
car wreck
dog/cat
waiter/customer
officer/criminal suspect
coach/athlete
hostage/kidnapper

Activity #3: A Bizarre Scene with Limitations

1. Divide a sheet of paper in half. On the left side, list as many bizarre character types as you can think of.

(Examples: bipolar baby sitter, one-eyed science teacher)

2. On the right side, list as many bizarre settings as you can think of.

(Examples: Santa's torture chamber, nightclub for white people who can't dance)

3. Now choose two of these characters and place them into one of your settings. Start writing, uninterrupted, for at least ten minutes.

4. Once you've made some headway into your scene, try to challenge yourself by adding the following restrictions at five minute intervals (after each interval, only the new restriction remains.)

Restriction #1: Make one of your characters really kind, and one of them really mean.

Restriction #2: Both of your characters are limited to no more than five words each time they talk.

Restriction #3: One character is limited to no more than two words each time they talk.

Restriction #4: Choose the first random object that comes into your view as you are writing. Within the next two lines of dialogue, incorporate this object as a prop in your scene.

Activity #4: Secret Revealed

1. Choose one of the following secrets that a character could possess:
- Sexual orientation
- Eating disorder
- Addiction of some kind
- Popular, used to be awkward
- Witness protection program
- Father in the mafia
- Abusive parent/boyfriend
- Can't read or can't dance

- Secretly in love with someone
- Cheated on way to success
- Lied about age
- Embarrassing obsession with some object
- Pregnancy

2. Now write a scene in which your character's secret is revealed against their will.

For example:

Secret: father in the mafia.

Revealed to: fiancé

Scene of Conflict: the final moments before a wedding

Activity # 5: Exposition Work

In order to write a full-length play, you must first create an exposition that describes your main characters as well as the layout of the stage. The following play concepts are tried and true, ranging everywhere from comedy to tragedy:

Love triangle/relationship

Speed dating

Abuse

War

Fish out of water

School/social stereotypes

Role reversals (i.e. gender, race, age, occupation, etc.)

Horror story

Schizophrenia

Devil/angel on shoulder

Satire of fairy tale or classic story

Hostage situation
Jerry Springer talk show

Activity #6: Satire of a Classic Story

Take a well-known story and rewrite a scene in contemporary form. Satire works extremely well on the stage because drama inherently exaggerates real life situations. Here are some good story concepts to pull from:

Snow White and the Seven Dwarves
Pinocchio
Cinderella
The Wizard of Oz
Romeo and Juliet
Peter Pan
The Hobbit
Winnie the Pooh
Beauty and the Beast
The Nutcracker
Alice in Wonderland
Little Red Riding Hood
Sleeping Beauty
Hansel and Gretel
The Odyssey
King Arthur and his Knights
Where the Wild Things Are
Charlie and the Chocolate Factory
Harry Potter
Twilight
Dr. Seuss

Chapter 6
Nonfiction

In this chapter, we will not be writing formal essays. Let me make that abundantly clear. Not that there's anything wrong with that kind of writing...actually, yes there is. I've gotta be honest here, if I have to grade another "In this essay I'm going to talk about..." paper I will probably set my hair on fire. I hate essays. I hated writing them in college. I hate reading them now.

So no, we will not be writing essays in this chapter.

Nonfiction is not boring. It is not bland. Truth is the most powerful form of writing, even with the understanding that all good fiction is indirectly true. We do not write in a vacuum. Every story that we create is inevitably shaped by our experiences, the people we've met, the places we've lived. And while fiction does have tremendous power, nonfiction – when it is done well – can teach us about the world in many exciting ways.

Activity #1: Belief Statement

I've borrowed the crux of this activity from National Public Radio. For years, NPR has invited normal, everyday people to write a belief statement, usually no longer than 250 words. It could be big picture, deeply personal, quirky, universal – anything goes. I've always been drawn to belief statements, in part because I have to read so many variations of them as my students apply for college. Unfortunately, they often have no idea what they believe, what they stand for, what makes them angry, or happy, or what moves them to tears. The power of a "This I Believe" piece lies in its brevity. Can you state your beliefs with power, with clarity, with an idea that resonates with others?

So what do you believe? Some of you will be off and running, while others may need a little help.

1. Start by answering one of the following questions: What makes you happy? What makes you sad? What do you puzzle about 'til your puzzler is sore? (to paraphrase the Grinch) Take your answer and run with it for 250 words.

2. Here's another approach: who or what is the strongest influence on your life? Is it a family member? An event from your past? Write about how this person or event has shaped you into the person you are today.

3. Maybe you need something a little more specific, something to push against. I like to give my students the following topics, and they have to take a stand about whether they agree or disagree with each statement:

Love #1 – Men and women can never truly be friends. Physical attraction will always get in the way.

Love #2 – Family love is stronger than romantic love.

Pain – Personal character cannot be developed without pain.

Faith – There is an all-knowing God watching over us.

Comfort – I regularly look for experiences to push me out of my comfort zone.

Beauty – Physical beauty fades over time.

Identity – When we are born, our basic personality (identity) has already been established.

Hope – When I think of the future, it is with more hope than fear.

Morality – There will always be evil in the world; it is inevitable.

Activity #2: The Memoir

A memoir differs from an autobiography in that it focuses on a specific time in a writer's life – the first year after moving to a new town, a life-changing summer, the aftershocks of a loved one's death, etc. Autobiographies serve a purpose, but they are often limited to the "what" in a person's life, from start to finish. A memoir captures the sights, the smells, the little moments that come alive on the page and carry us along for the ride.

So how do we choose what matters most? Here are some possibilities:

1. On a sheet of paper, write the age in your life that you feel like you grew or changed the most. Circle that age, and in the space surrounding that number, write everything that you associate with that specific age – all the people who affected you, the highs, the lows, the songs that played on repeat in your head.

2. What kind of a history do you carry with you? Answer each of the following prompts in ten minutes of uninterrupted writing.
   - I come from…
   - I come from a family…

3. Tell the story of your name. Were you named for someone? Do you know how or why your name was chosen? Does your name reflect a particular ethnicity? Has your name changed? How do you feel about your name?

4. Remember a place that was important to you when you were younger – literally walk a friend through this place, painting a picture with your words and your hand gestures. Tell them what you can smell, taste, see, hear, and feel. Then grab a sketch pad and draw this place from memory. When you are done, step back and look at your drawing. Does it do justice to the picture in your head? Probably not. Now take a half hour and "draw" this place with your words, adding sensory details to give it depth and dimension. Think of all the limitations of a two dimensional sketch and use this as motivation to bring your special place to life. Make it sing, give it a full palette of colors, add some conversations that

you've had in this place (you thought you were done with dialogue, did you not? It is like weeds in the cracks of a concrete path.)

5. Go online and listen to any number of live storytelling shows that have gained popularity in recent years (*The Moth Radio Hour*, *Snap Judgement*, and *The Monti* are three of my favorites.) Pay attention to the kinds of stories that these regular, everyday people tell. Now imagine that you have ten minutes on stage to tell a story of your own. What would it be about? How would you structure the narrative arc? What would the payoff be at the end?

Activity #3: Telling Someone Else's Story

Everyone has a powerful story to tell. When we interview someone, how do we pull that powerful story out, bringing it to life in all of its beauty and wonder? It's all about asking the right questions.

I like to illustrate this point in class with a simple introductory activity. Two students come to the front of the room, and I give them a picture to look at (usually the classic Andy Warhol painting of Marilyn Monroe or one of M.C. Escher's more complex sketches.) These two students have to describe the picture to the class, and the class will try to recreate the sketch solely based on the description provided. The class is encouraged to ask follow-up questions about what the image looks like. The results are predictably all over the place, depending on the clarity of the questions and the level of detail in the descriptions. The same holds true with an interview. We, the interviewee, begin with a blank canvas in our mind. When we interview someone, this person begins to fill our blank canvas with the colors and details of their story. But if we don't ask the right questions, the canvas remains incomplete, a mere shell of its reality.

So for this activity, get someone to tell you a story about their life. Ask questions and listen carefully to the details they provide, all the while painting a picture in your head. Pay attention to the gaps and fill them in with follow-up questions. Focus on sensory details, particularly sounds and smells. Be prepared for the unexpected. More often than not, you will be pleasantly surprised by the final result.

I used this process extensively in my book *A World Beyond Home*, which features the life stories of several of my former students. In the following excerpt, I underlined and placed in bold the original details I collected from one of my interviews. Victoria told me an interesting story from her life, but the details were very sparse. By asking her specific follow-up questions, I was able to create a much more fully realized picture for the reader. Here's the final version with the new details added in:

A World Beyond Home excerpt:
(the original story is **underlined** and in **bold**)

<u>Victoria Henderson sat with her head down in Ms. Weiss' 7th grade class, trying to disappear into the desk. It made her sad to see her classmates talking so comfortably in small clicks,</u> the cute boys in their long white t's never looking her way, all the accents so different from what she was used to.

She wanted to make at least one friend, just someone to talk to, someone to make her feel like she wasn't completely alone. But every time she thought about opening her mouth, she remembered what they said to her on that first day of school.

"Damn, girl, you talk like you're white."

The words caught Victoria off guard and wiped the smile right off of her face.

Two horrible months had passed since that first day of school. Moving to Durham wasn't so bad; as the child of military parents, she was used to being the new kid. She'd already lived in New Jersey, Texas, Germany, Pennsylvania, and Rhode Island. But this was her first time living away from a military base. **They'd gotten a modest brick apartment in Yorktown. Not the best place to live, but not the worst either.** Victoria was used to playing with kids like her who'd traveled around the world. Living on a military base, everyone's dad was a master sergeant major. Everyone made the same amount of money. Class and race didn't really matter. She could run around the base and know that she was safe. She never cared about criticism. When she wanted something, she went for it. No hesitation.

So why was she hesitating now? Who cared if she had a New England accent? Why did it matter?

Victoria did her best to fit in. Up in Rhode Island, nobody cared about brand names. If you had clean clothes on your back, you were good to go. But when she walked into Githens Middle School on that first day, they ripped her apart for wearing Sketchers without the "S" - and from Walmart, too. Here in Durham it was all about Rocawear velour suits for the girls, long white t's and crisp Air Force Ones for the boys. Style mattered, and if you didn't have it, you were nobody. **Victoria experimented with her hair and tried to wear some of the new styles as best she could, but they still wouldn't talk to her.**

In the desk ahead of her, DJ was clowning around as usual. He was one of the few people who talked to Victoria, but he talked to everybody, so that really didn't count. But when he *did* talk to her, she didn't feel quite so lonely. All she had to do was open her mouth. What else was she gonna do, stare at the desk all year long? Her mother had raised her to be stronger than that.

But in middle school, you don't just walk up to a boy and talk to him. You gotta have a reason. You gotta strut the right way, hold your head high, swing your hips to get his attention. You gotta be sexy. As a 7th grader, this was all foreign to Victoria, but so many of the girls were already talking this way, walking this way. You had to be beautiful to get attention. And if you weren't blessed with good looks - at least in the eyes of a middle school boy - you had to pull the wool over their eyes with a sexy glance, a twist, something, anything, because if the boys didn't like you, you were nothing. That's the way things worked around here.

Victoria tried to think of something to say to DJ. He was kinda cute, seemed to know everybody. Ms. Weiss was taking attendance or something, but Victoria wasn't listening. She was thinking about one thing and one thing only: not being alone.

DJ was wylin' out like always, throwing paper balls around the room, kicking the desk of the girl next to him. She rolled her eyes and adjusted her purple Rocawear suit, but she smiled at him anyway.

Now was the time. Victoria still couldn't think of anything to say. Maybe she should just keep her mouth shut. DJ turned to the front of the room. Victoria leaned forward, gathered her courage, and swatted him in the back of the head.

DJ stood still for a moment. Then he rolled his shoulders forward as if he was shaking off a fly. **He got out of his desk and stood above Victoria.** Before she could even smile, he punched her square in the face.

The air seemed to get sucked out of the room. As Victoria fell to the floor, that almost-smile was still at the edge of her lips. **She crumpled into a ball, closed her eyes and covered her head. She tried not to cry.**

DJ stood over her, along with the rest of the class. They weren't happy, really, but they weren't sad either. It just confirmed what they already knew about the new girl.

Victoria's humiliation was complete.

(As you can see, Victoria's story is not nearly as effective without the follow-up details. This process takes time, and it may require some trial and error to tease out the kinds of details you need. But the end result is a fully realized story.)

Activity #4: Humans of (Your Home Town)

This activity borrows from the blog and bestselling book *Humans of New York*. Go out into your community and find someone who looks interesting to you. Take a picture of them in a pose of their choice, one that accentuates their distinct personality. Then interview them using the techniques in Activity #3. Print off a copy of their picture and write your narrative version of their story. Now do this with at least five other people to create a visual profile of your city's inhabitants. This activity will help you to see the humanity in people by asking the right questions and getting to know someone on a deeper level.

Activity #5: Humanizing a person or event

This activity blurs the line between fiction and nonfiction. Narrative nonfiction uses the storytelling techniques of fiction (such as dialogue and internal thoughts) to tell a true story in a creative way.

1. Create a list of famous people and events on a sheet of paper. Try to include a combination of both recent and historical.

2. Choose one of these famous people to write a personalized portrait of an event in that person's life (for example, a profile of JFK in the moments leading up to his assassination.)

3. Now choose one of your events, and imagine a person who could have appeared in this event, trying to be as true to

the factual details of that event as possible (for example, an American soldier on D-Day as he storms the beach at Normandy.)

This activity, if done well, requires a significant amount of historical research. You want to get the details right whenever possible. If you're writing about 9/11, listen to the cockpit recordings of United Airlines Flight 93 and absorb the actual words of the terrorists. Learn about the Holocaust by reading the journals of Jewish prisoners. Listen to MLK's speech on the Washington lawn and study the crowds gaping up at him in picture after picture. Become an expert on your subject and then bring your subject to life.

Narrative nonfiction is a powerful way to make history seem tangible. What was going through Nixon's head in the moments after he resigned from the presidency? As Saddam Hussein stood beneath the gallows, was he scared? Defiant? Truth can be just as pleasurable to read as fiction, when it is done well.

Activity #6: Culture Piece

Think of a place from your past that consisted of a wide array of people. Schools work well for this activity, particularly middle school because it is such a turbulent time in the lives of most adolescents. But you could also choose a neighborhood, a place of employment, or a summer camp. Now make a list of distinct details about this place so that an outsider can get a vivid picture of it. Divide these details into the following categories:

1. physical details – Avoid generalizations as much as possible. We all know that your classroom hallways had concrete walls and dingy tiles. But what did the hallways smell like? What kind of graffiti was written on the bathroom walls?

2. culture – What were the hierarchies in this place? What were the cliques? Which groups didn't get along with each other?

3. characters – Who were the most memorable "characters" in this place you are describing?

Now write about a memorable event that you witnessed in this place. It could be funny, heartbreaking, or embarrassing. Whatever it is, really try to bring this place to life using physical description, cultural hierarchies, and character development.

Activity #7: Humor Piece

What makes something funny? Ask ten people and they will give you ten different answers. Some people like satire. Other people like slapstick humor or corny jokes. But there's one kind of humor that most people can generally agree on: self-parody.

People gravitate to writers who can make fun of themselves. It shows that they are comfortable in their own skin, that they are slow to anger and quick to show empathy for someone else's quirks.

This activity is inspired by the blog "Stuff White People Like." I use this example because I am a white person, and if you are going to do an activity like this, you have to make fun of a group that you identify with. "Stuff White People Like" is a popular blog because it focuses on the strange things that white people identify with. For example: assists in basketball (white people are typically slow and thus pass the ball to more athletic players to score.)

1. Choose a group that you identify with. It doesn't have to be about race or gender. It could be "Stuff Southerners Like" or Stuff Blond Girls Like." Whatever. Don't go for the obvious stereotypes either. When you make fun of yourself, you are also celebrating the distinct characteristics of your own group.

2. Come up with a list of 20 "things" that your group likes.

3. Now write a humor piece about a few of these things, providing light-hearted examples along the way. Remember that this is an act of self-parody. Be willing to make fun of yourself.

Want to take a riskier approach to humor writing? Try the following activity:

1. Make a list of things that frustrate or annoy you. Place them into three categories: people, places, and situations.

2. Choose one of these ideas and write a rant about what makes this person, place, or situation so annoying. Be careful to avoid being mean-spirited. Lean on self-parody once again. Really exaggerate your annoyance. Stand-up comedians use this technique all the time.

Activity #8: The Critique

We've all heard the cliché that "everyone's a critic." And in the ever-changing world of social media, this is definitely true. But bashing something you don't like (or even praising it), doesn't make you an effective critic. Now more than ever, the world needs people who can respond to the world around them with honesty, clarity, and intelligence.

Choose one of the following areas to critique:

1. Movie – In your critique of a specific movie, focus on the acting, the storyline, and the cinematography.

2. Music – This is perhaps the most difficult art form to be objective. If we don't like country music, for example, it is hard for us to cast aside our biases about country music to give a song or album an objective assessment. But try to approach this with an open mind. Focus on the instruments, the lyrics, the quality of the singing. Close your eyes and give it multiple listens before passing judgment.

3. Food – Use all five senses to describe a particular dining experience. Like music, try to approach each entrée with an open mind.

You can blend any one of these three critiques into a memoir piece as well. What was the soundtrack of your life in middle school? What foods conjure up memories from your past? What movie heroes did you aspire to be as a kid? The possibilities are endless.

Chapter 7
Children's/Young Adult

What books did you read growing up? What made good books so good?

Sometimes we take this fundamental question for granted. In our rush to impress readers with dazzling metaphors and sophisticated prose, we sometimes abandon the pure, unadulterated joy of storytelling. We forget the child-like wonder of falling headlong into a world where animals talk and the landscape is filled with vibrant colors.

Ralph Waldo Emerson speaks to this child-like wonder in his essay "Nature," creating a fitting metaphor for the creative process as a whole. "Few adult persons can see nature," Emerson writes. "At least they have a very superficial seeing. The sun illuminates only the eye of the man, but shines into the eye and the heart of the child. The lover of nature is he whose inward and outward senses are still truly adjusted to each other; who has retained the spirit of infancy even into the era of manhood."

When we write for children and young adults, we have a chance to regain this child-like wonder in our own stories.

I have two young sons, and every night I see this wonder come to life as we read stories together. Whether it's Dr. Seuss, Mo Willems, the classics as well as the quirky new books – it really doesn't matter. My boys will sit there for hours if I let them, listening to these stories well into the night and loving every minute of it. And as I sit there with them, flying along to new worlds and laughing at the same lines again and again, my heart grows three sizes larger than it was the day before.

Many writers believe that you have to dumb down your ideas when you write for children, but that's not entirely true. "Simple" and "simplistic" are not the same concepts. "Simple" implies clear, vivid prose that connects with young readers. "Simplistic" condescends to the lowest common denominator. Yes, children need clear, simple sentences, but they also want to read stories with depth. Like adults (and at times, even more than adults,) they can spot a shallow storyline a mile away.

Activity #1: Adolescent Interests

Make a timeline of adolescent interests, starting with age three and moving across the page to middle school. Some of your items will probably be gender specific. As you create this chart, think about some of the following questions: When do children start to begin imaginative play? When does a child form his first real friendship?

Once this timeline is complete, decide which age group is the most interesting to you. This will help you determine the target audience for your children's book.

Activity #2: Lessons for our Youth

Think about the young people you encounter on a regular basis – your cousins, neighbors, the screaming child in the checkout line at Walmart. Now make a list of the lessons that children aren't being taught well in our society today. There are a million books out there about sharing, but what about bullying, or body image? The children's literature market is very difficult to break into as a writer, in part because there are only so many lessons that we can teach. So go for something a bit off the beaten path and let the clarity of your story win the day.

Activity #3: Simplifying Style

Grab a book that is filled with dense vocabulary and complex prose. I like to use the opening paragraph from David Guterson's novel *Snow Falling on Cedars* for this activity, but any book will do. Now try to rewrite a paragraph from this book so that an 11 year old could understand it. What words would you have to replace? What entire phrases would you completely rework? This activity will be challenging enough, but if you really want to push yourself, try to do the same thing by rewriting this paragraph so that a five year old will be able to understand it.

Remember, you're not trying to "dumb down" the text – you're simplifying it instead.

Activity #4: Make a Fortune in YA

You can always forget about writing children's books and go for the most lucrative genre in publishing today: young adult literature (YA.) Books such as *Divergent*, *The Hunger Games*, *Twilight*, and *The Fault in our Starts* have made an absolute killing in recent years, and the race is on for the next big series (the word *series* is important because YA branding really drives book sales and, of course, the movie tie-ins down the road.) But while there's money to be made in YA lit, millions of writers are scrambling to be the next Suzanne Collins. The competition is stiff, so enter at your own risk.

I'm just glad to see young people reading. And while dystopian novels and star-crossed love affairs are wearing thin, the Young Adult market has plenty of room to grow. I'm still waiting for a YA book that tackles race, immigration, or LGBT issues in a compelling way. How about religion? Or xenophobia? The best books force us to ask big questions, the kinds of questions with no easy answers but enough substance to make us consider the world in all of its complexity. Young people want to wade into these waters. They're just waiting for someone to provide the spark.

Chapter 8
Screenplay Writing

Screenplay writing is tailor-made for the control freak in all of us. Like playwriting, dialogue serves as the primary narrative device in a screenplay. But when you write for film, you control everything – the ironic tone of the dialogue, the close camera angle on a character's face, the heavy orchestral music playing in the background, literally everything. If you want an audience to *see* something, you better include it in your screenplay or else it's never going to appear.

In screenplay writing, the way you format your document is extremely important. If you want your screenplay to be taken seriously, you need to follow every rule closely – character names ALL CAPS and centered, EXT to indicate the beginning of an outside scene, one page of script is roughly equivalent to one minute of film, et cetera. There are plenty of resources out there for these endless rules, so read up and don't deviate from a single one of them.

For the sake of this book, I am not going to dwell on the finer points of screenplay formatting. We'll stick with the big picture here. If you decide to write a screenplay, you should ask yourself the following questions:

1. Is it possible to translate my story concept from the written page into a feature-length film?

2. Is there a market for my film?

3. Does my story follow the traditional narrative arc that we've come to expect in a movie (a character wants something, overcomes an obstacle, and then gets what he/she wants in the end)?

If you can answer *yes* to all three questions, go for it. But go for it knowing that Hollywood is a fickle beast (not unlike the publishing industry.) If something is hot, then every producer in the country wants to see scripts that fall into this same vein (brooding vampire hunks! Children killing each other in a dystopian world! Derivative remakes!)

Activity #1: Adapting your story into a screenplay

One way to approach screenplay writing is to take a story or novel you have already written and adapt it into a screenplay. For curiosity's sake, you can also take an existing novel and create a rough adaptation, but keep in mind that you will ultimately have to get permission from the author to have this book made into a film.

Consider the following steps when adapting a story into a screenplay:

1. Make sure that you are intimately familiar with the story. What does it *feel* like? What is the tone? Try to anticipate some of the challenges that will come when you carry that tone from the page to the screen.

2. Pinpoint the 6 or 7 scenes that stick in your mind the most. Let these scenes be the foundation that you build your movie around.

3. Try to summarize each scene of your film into 1-2 sentences. Once you have done this, read through this outline to see if your plot has effective pacing. Is this a gripping story? Will moviegoers want to stick around until the end? What feels like fluff and what is absolutely essential to the story?

4. Decide who is the main character of your story. Is it a single, tragic hero? Does your plot revolve around multiple characters? Your answers will determine the focus of your film.

5. Now think about the ending. Does it need to be more visual? Does it leave a lasting impression on the viewer?

6. You also need to think about the beginning. Does it draw us in right away? Just like a effective story, a movie should open by immediately throwing us into the action. Grab us from the opening sequence and don't let up until the final credits role.

7. As you think through all of these points, be open to reworking the story in significant ways. Most movie adaptations have to cut a number of plot points from their source material. Otherwise, a movie would be at least ten hours long (of course, if you're going for a TV series that unfolds over the course of a season, this could work to your advantage.) Regardless, there will be subplots that need to be cut, combined, or reordered to fit the needs of your screenplay.

8. Which characters have to go? As you cut down your plot, some of your characters will be cast aside as well. Don't despair; this is all part of the process.

9. One of the biggest challenges of going from a written story to film is the use of internal thoughts. How will you translate the internal into the external? Use voice-overs sparingly.

10. Some scenes in your story may need to be expanded, particularly if the source material is a short story or novella. But be careful here; you don't want to create a scene just to fill a hole, because the audience will sniff it out.

Adapting a story is a complicated task. You may or may not be able to stay faithful to the original story. You may have to remove some of your best material in order to stay true to the story. But even if you decide that screenplay writing isn't for you, going through this process can be extremely valuable.

A reader creates a movie in her head as she reads through our story. Her life experiences and her current state of mind will shape this movie, but the writer ultimately determines whether she keeps reading or if she turns off the lights and goes to bed for the night.

Chapter 9
Writing Outside of Yourself

My students were silent as I stepped away from the whiteboard and allowed the words I had just written to sink in:

The Self

The Outside World

The Effective Writer

"Is it really possible for a writer to be objective?" I asked after a short pause.

"Sure it is," said a girl in the front row. Her name was Martha. Always eager, always tapping her pen with nervous energy.

"Go on," I said.

"I mean, a writer has to lose herself in the story, to let it take on a life of its own. It's not about you; it's about the facts."

"I disagree," said a student in the back. It was Devin, the classic contrarian. He loved to get a rise out of others, to argue for the sake of arguing. "We can't abandon our biases, even when we write about someone else."

"So we use our biases as a crutch?" I asked him.

"Not a crutch. It's just human nature."

"So let me ask you this," I said to the class as a whole. "In order to be an effective writer, do you need to understand the outside world as well as the inner workings of your own heart?"

"The heart and the mind are two completely different issues," interrupted Martha.

"Yes they are," I replied. "But the heart is the driving force of our thoughts. How can we write if we don't understand our own motivations?"

"And how can we understand our own motivations if we shield ourselves from the outside world?" Devin chimed in again.

I nodded my head slowly. "Which leads us to a bigger issue. I'm a human being. I breathe, I think, I feel. When I put pen to paper, I channel my worldview in subtle and unexpected ways. William Faulkner was on to something when he said that the past is never dead. It's not even past. Everything we do or say holds the imprint of our own identity."

I usually have this debate with my students at the end of the school year. To be a great writer, I ask them, do we need to understand ourselves as well as the outside world? They disagree on the relationship between the two, but one point becomes very clear: it is impossible to grow as a writer unless you engage in the outside world.

This does not diminish the life of the mind. Or memoir writing. Or the role of our psychology in all that we create. But it *is* an acknowledgement of our own limitations.

In my book *A World Beyond Home*, I explored why some students drift into adulthood while others transition into a stable job and a rich inner life. The answer was pretty clear. Successful students, I learned, found a passion outside of their daily experiences and pursued this passion throughout high school. After high school, this passion led them to explore the world outside of their hometown, and when they explored the world outside of their hometown, they met people who expanded their view of what it means to be an adult. Here was the real tipping point: once their minds were open to new people and new ideas, they became more empathetic human beings. The world didn't revolve around them anymore; it revolved around others.

Empathy and curiosity are powerful tools for any writer. When we are interested in the world outside of ourselves, our stories take on a broader scope. We don't run out of ideas. Our characters are more fully realized. Everything we write has more depth.

Activity #1: Cataloguing your focus as a writer

1. Make a list of 5 things that make you happy, and then 5 things that make you angry. Then make a list of 5 topics that make you think deeply.

2. For each of these three lists, rank your items from most to least personal. Now think about how this list has evolved

as you've gotten older. In a sense, you have just completed a quick scan of your brain. This is what makes you tick as a human being.

3. Now make a list of the stories or poems you have written in the past year. Are there any reoccurring topics or themes in your writing? If so, this will give you a window into the kind of ideas that are running through your head. If there doesn't seem to be any rhyme or reason to what you chose to write about, don't be alarmed. This could be an indication that you are already willing to look outside of yourself to create something fresh and original.

Activity #2: Using sensory experiences to drive your creativity

There are a few simple ways to prod your brain to look outside of its normal channels for inspiration.

1. Listen to the soundtrack from a movie that you haven't seen before. While you are listening to a song, make a word map of every thought or image that comes into your head, solely based on the tone of the music. I like to use several different styles of music, such as the theme song from a bank-heist movie called *The Town*, as well as the opening track from a Bollywood movie called *Monsoon Wedding*. Compare the images from these two very different soundtracks to see just how much the tone of a song can push your creativity in different directions.

2. If you prefer something more visual, look at the opening scene of a movie – I highly recommend the first four minutes of *Garden State*, but any movie will do – and then write for 15 minutes, using this clip as inspiration for some piece of creativity. It could be a story, a poem, a play, whatever works for you.

3. Once you have done this activity, think about the following question: How easy was it for you to take an outside sensory experience and use it for your own creativity? Your answer will say a lot about your willingness to bring the outside world into your writing.

Activity #3: Getting inspiration from other people

This activity is simple but very effective:

1. Talk to a friend who knows a lot about something that is completely foreign to you.

2. Interview your friend to learn as much as you possibly can about this subject, and then try to incorporate this new knowledge into a story.

Most novelists use this method extensively. In my novel *Bull City*, one of the most important scenes takes place in an interrogation room. I knew very little about police procedures, so I interviewed a homicide detective who worked as a resource officer at my school. Not only did his insights make the scene more realistic (the good cop, bad cop thing really is an effective interrogation technique), but the interview gave me some ideas that I never would have considered otherwise.

While I was talking to this detective, he had a toothpick perched precariously on the edge of his lips. I kept staring at the toothpick as he talked, waiting for it to fall to the table, but it never did. I was able to incorporate this detail into my scene, with the murder suspect driven nearly crazy by the toothpick dangling on the edge of his interrogator's lips. The image added a great deal of tension to the scene, and I never would have used it if I hadn't talked to the detective in the first place.

Films about Writing and Creativity

If you want some more great ideas to spur your writing, look no further than these excellent films:

Dead Poet's Society – Robin Williams plays a boarding school teacher who inspires his students to think independently through reading and writing poetry. The ending is chilling and will stay with you for days.

Freedom Writers – This movie is based on the real life story of Erin Gruwell, a teacher at an inner city school who transforms her students by asking them to write their life stories. Gruwell eventually published these stories in a bestselling book called the *Freedom Writer's Diary*, which was the basis for the film.

Shattered Glass – A true story based on the controversial rise and fall of journalist Stephen Glass, who fabricated numerous stories for the *New Republic* before he was eventually caught. Glass's story is a cautionary tale about fame and journalistic ethics.

Finding Forrester – Based loosely on the lives of Ralph Ellison and J.D. Salinger, this tale of a reclusive writer who mentors a brilliant young basketball player/writer does a masterful job of entertaining us while still providing some valuable insights about the writing process.

Limitless – Bradley Cooper plays Eddie Morra, a struggling writer who happens upon a mysterious drug that gives him almost superhuman mental powers. While not a perfect film, *Limitless* poses some provocative questions about creativity and artistic success.

Chapter 10
The Importance of Reading

Reading is a dying art. At least it seems that way when I talk to my students.

So many of them loved books when they were younger, but high school seems to have killed that love. We ask them to analyze a book to death, squeezing the life out of a text to find the symbols and the deeper meanings. We pile so many assignments on them that the simple act of reading for pleasure has disappeared.

Just read the CliffsNotes summary and be done with it, they say to me.

We can blame social media for their shortened attention spans, but they *are* reading constantly (whether a tweet or a Snapchat story actually enhances or deadens the brain is up for debate.)

So why read?

How does it help our writing?

For starters, all the best writers are voracious readers. They find their voice by mimicking the voices of others, absorbing another writer's style and trying it on like a new pair of pants, manipulating the tone and structure until it sounds true to who they are.

And that's just the start.

When we read widely, we open our minds to the outside world. You can start with the classics, but you should read popular fiction as well. Even if the storylines are formulaic and the characters are thinly drawn, these books will show you what the great masses want to read. Don't be a snob about it; we can learn from the simple as well as the complex.

Our brain is like a muscle, and as with any exercise, we must stimulate our muscles in different ways. Otherwise our thoughts get stuck in a rut. We find ourselves above the fray, too good for "those" books, looking down on the common people who will never be as good as us.

So read widely. And challenge yourself as well. Keep an open mind about a subject that you never would have considered to be interesting. More often than not you will discover a passage that helps you to see the world with fresh eyes.

Books are like people in this way.

When we first meet a stranger, we often make judgments about this person based solely on the way he carries himself. But over time we begin to dig deeper. We learn about his past, his pet peeves, the good and bad experiences that have shaped who he is. We begin to see this person in a whole new light. It's often a kick to the gut – I judged you and I was wrong; I made an assumption, and you know what they say about assumptions…

And so it is with books. A good book will surprise you, move you, enlighten you. The daily act of reading will calm your scattered thoughts and organize your fragmented world. Reading will inspire you to pick up a pen and write like your very existence depends on it.

Chapter 11
Novel Writing

When I finish a good book, my first thought is, *I wish I could have written that.*

When I finish a bad book, my first thought is, *I could write something better than that.*

You've probably been there too. Perhaps the next great American novel is sitting in your head, just waiting to be transcribed into a Word document and released to the world, bringing you fame and fortune and The Good Life. Or maybe you don't care about fame. Let's be honest, very few writers make a living at this anyway. But there's something to be said about finishing a book, about leaving something tangible to those who come after us.

Over the past ten years, 50 of my students have completed full-length novels. Some of these books are extremely well-written, and some of them are not. Countless other students began their great American novel in my class but gave up long before they reached the finish line.

Writing a novel is the ultimate challenge. You have to live with a set of characters for weeks on end, shaping them and carrying them through an increasingly complex web of events. Some days the words spill onto the page with a rush. These are the days we live for – the exhilaration, the sense of purpose, the feeling that we can do anything.

And then the next day we sit down in the same seat with the same optimism, and everything we write is simply awful. We hate our characters and we hate ourselves for thinking that we had what it takes to write a book in the first place. What were we thinking?! We're tempted to throw the laptop skyward and laugh maniacally as it shatters into a million pieces. And good riddance. Why write when there are a million more fulfilling hobbies out there?

But you won't throw the laptop. At least I hope you won't. You'll keep your butt firmly situated in the seat and think back to yesterday when the writing came so naturally. You'll remind yourself that the muse will come again. Maybe not tomorrow or the next day. But the inspiration will return in due time.

Most of the great satisfactions in life can only occur when we first experience discomfort. We have to work for what we want. We have to climb the mountain by foot instead of driving to the summit. Sometimes it hurts. Sometimes it's a grind. But you have to be persistent. When I feel like I'm about to pull my hair out, I often think of these words from the journalist William Zinsser: "I don't like to write, but I love to have written."

Don't get discouraged if your book doesn't make you rich and famous. When you write to please others, your writing loses much or what makes it unique and original. Instead, write for the satisfaction of knowing that you have created something entirely new in the world, something that will be a legacy when your time on this earth has come and gone.

Activity #1: Brainstorming ideas for your novel

Let's say you want to write a book but you have absolutely no idea where to begin. This activity will help you to tap into the fabric of your own life. Start by writing what you know and move on from there.

1. List the 5 defining moments of your life so far.

2. List the 5 defining people in your life.

3. List 5 subjects outside of your daily life that fascinate you.

4. Now take a look at these three lists and think about which items have the most plot possibilities.

Can one of your defining moments be shaped into a scene of conflict?

Can one of the defining people in your life be morphed into a character, or can you blend some of the traits from different people into a single character?

The topics in List #3 probably have the most potential to be tapped into. If you write about something that fascinates you, that interest will shine through in your work. Readers will care about your topic because *you* care about the topic. (On that note, if a scene feels boring to you while you write it, you can safely assume that it will bore the reader as well.)

5. Free write on any of these topics for at least 15 minutes. If you like where it's going, keep writing; if not, cast it aside and move on to something else.

Activity #2: Developing your story ideas through newspaper headlines

Scan through a newspaper and look at the headlines. Your best bets will be human interest profiles instead of the major news stories of the day. As you read these headlines, try to imagine the fictional possibilities for some of them. Television shows use this process all the time (think *Law and Order's* "Ripped from the Headlines" episodes, for example.) Some of the most successful authors in the world use this method as well, creating complex, sprawling novels out of a single headline. You can even keep a notebook full of headlines and pull from them when you are running low on ideas. Real life is often stranger than fiction. Don't be afraid to use it for inspiration.

Activity #3: Developing your characters

Revisit the character prompts from Chapter 3. Try to create multiple characters and place them side by side. Do you see them as rivals? Siblings? Lovers? If they were to meet for the first time, where would the scene take place?

What would happen to them? Remember that well-developed characters will drive the plot of your book.

Activity #4: Setting and point of view

In Chapter 3, we did a zooming activity with a toll booth operator at the George Washington Bridge. This activity is a helpful way to introduce the setting of a novel. It will force you to consider several things:

1. When we first meet your main character, what does the reader see? How do we want our character to look? How much of their personality do we reveal with their actions or internal thoughts?

2. What about the setting? Do we begin with a close-up or a wide, panoramic view?

3. Should we begin with action to draw the reader in? Perhaps our setting is vivid enough on its own.

Consider all of these questions, because once you lose the reader's attention you will have a hard time winning it back.

Here's an example of the zooming technique from my novel *Bull City*. In this scene I've introduced both the main character of the book and a setting that plays an integral role in the story **[with commentary inserted into the text]:**

[wide view] The city of Boston sparkled with late spring sunshine. **[zoom in]** A Red Line subway car emerged from the city's underbelly and rose above the Charles River. **[zoom in]** Construction workers heading to the Big Dig downtown sat side by side with families on their way to the frigid waters of Revere Beach. Every passenger took in the breathtaking view of Back Bay, Beacon Hill, and the imposing skyscrapers of the city. **[pan across]** A subway car passing in the opposite direction momentarily blocked their view. This car was filled with people heading to MIT's dim, modern buildings along the Charles River. To the west, MIT soon gave way to the tree-lined campus of Harvard, America's most venerable university and the crown jewel of New England's intellectual elite.

[zoom out] The city hummed with pent-up energy from the long, cold months that had just passed. **[zoom in]** Rap music filled the streets, mixed with the meringue beats of a 1970s-era Monte Carlo dangling the white cross of the Dominican flag from its rearview mirror. **[pan across]** Along this stretch of the Charles River, Harvard Crimson crew captains shouted instructions to a synchronized team of rowers. Coeds sat on the grassy banks with cell phones and textbooks in hand. **[pan across]** Farther down the river, the Greek columns and ivy walls of Harvard's football stadium surrounded a freshly cut field. The city was quiet here.

[transition from setting to character] A young man bounded up the concrete bleachers of Harvard Stadium two at a time, creating a jagged shadow. He was breathing heavily, and his lean, taught forearms pumped with the precision of a well-oiled piston. He wore a retro Boston Celtics jersey and black mesh shorts which sagged below his knees. **[tight zoom]** A tiny circle of quartz glimmered from his left ear; his eyes were utterly calm. It was a striking image, a young man straining harder with every step, muscles tense, mouth twitching, with intense green eyes that seemed to be completely disconnected from the rest of his body.

Overview of the publishing industry

So you've completed the great American novel and you think you are ready for publication. The process is pretty straightforward, but it is extremely difficult. If you want to get your book published by a mainstream press, you need to follow these steps:

1. Get an agent.

Agents are the gate keepers to publishing companies, and it is nearly impossible to get published without first gaining representation. Agents make their money when you get an advance from a publishing company. *Never pay an agent for their services.* There are plenty of shady characters out there who are more than happy to take your money. Agents get paid when you get paid, never before.

2. Write an effective query letter.

This is your introduction to agents, so take your time and follow this format:

Paragraph One – The Hook: Write a concise, one-sentence tagline for your book. The hook should draw the reader in and make them want to learn more.

Paragraph Two – Mini-synopsis: Take the entire plot of your novel and condense it into about 200 words. This is no easy task, and you will probably have to write at least five drafts of this one paragraph. Introduce your main characters and some of the conflicts they will encounter. Let your distinct style shine through here. Publishers often use this summary to create the back cover copy for a book, so look at the back flaps of your favorite novels to see how this can be done.

Paragraph Three – Writer's Bio: This should be the easiest paragraph in your query to write. Be concise here, limiting yourself to biographical details related to writing. Agents like to see previous publication in magazines, newsletters, and literary journals.

Your Closing: Be sure to thank the agent for their time. If your book is fiction, offer to send along your full manuscript. If your book is nonfiction, be prepared to send a detailed outline and book proposal as well as the full manuscript.

Here's an example of the query letter I used for my novel *Bull City* (you can find many other examples of effective queries with a quick search online):

Dear Ms. _____:

After a night of club-hopping and cocaine, a Pakistani woman winds up dead in a fast-food dumpster. No one misses her. No one really cares that she's filled with bullet holes. But when an African-American homeless man discovers the body and is immediately charged with murder, a series of shocking events nearly bring a proud Southern city to its knees. *Bull City*, my debut novel, is both a mystery and a character study of "post-racial" America.

Bull City blends mystery and literary fiction in much the same way as Dennis Lehane's *Gone Baby Gone* and David Gutterson's *Snow Falling on Cedars*. I would be happy to send you the entire finished manuscript (85,250 words) if you are interested. Thank you very much for your time and consideration.

In addition to *Bull City*, I am the author of two memoirs – *Blessed Returns* and *Sidelines*, and I have written for the *Herald-Sun* (Durham, NC) and the *News and Observer* (Raleigh, NC.) I hold a degree in Creative Writing from UNC Chapel Hill and a M.Ed. from Harvard. For the past nine years, I've taught English and Creative Writing at a public high school in Durham, NC, where I received the Milken National Educator Award. In addition to teaching, I am a freelance editor and a regular guest lecturer across the Southeast on issues of urban education.

Sincerely yours,
Stuart Albright

The Next Step

Research agents in your genre and submit to as many as possible (www.agentquery.com is a great resource.) Don't get discouraged by rejection letters; you will get many of them. Agents are human, and they have particular tastes and relationships with specific publishers. They may like your novel concept about dogs but reject your query because they don't know any publishers who like dogs. You have to find the right fit, and this process takes time.

As far as word count goes, publishers generally look for novels between 70,000-100,000 words and memoirs between 50,000-80,000 words. If you have written a young adult novel, you can get away with 40,000 words, although the YA market is growing in sophistication and expected length – think *Harry Potter* et al.

So let's say you get an agent, and the agent gets you a book deal with a big New York publisher. You're set for life, right?

Wrong.

Advances can be as small as $1,000 and as large as $100,000 (there are outliers, of course – *City on Fire*, a debut novel by Garth Risk Hallberg recently sold for a reported $2 million, but a deal like this is *very* rare.) Some publishers will only pay royalties when your book has sold up to the amount of your advance. Major retailers will eat your royalties alive, leaving you with a kick back of $1-$2 for every book sold. Sadly, you probably can't quit your day job even if you get picked up by a major press.

There are other options, of course. Smaller independent presses often do not award advances at all, but they do provide regional distribution and get your book into "brick and mortar" stores such as Barnes and Noble and, well, that's about the only brick and mortar left, except for the few remaining independent book stores. By the way, support these independent book stores whenever possible – they are passionate about books, they support local writers, and they are about the only thing keeping Amazon and Barnes and Noble from completely monopolizing the publishing industry.

You can also bypass the traditional model all together to get your book published. Vanity presses will publish your book for a hefty fee. Companies like CreateSpace and Lulu provide more of a do-it-yourself (DIY) model if you're willing to put in the time to learn the finer points of interior design, cover design, and marketing (of course, even the biggest publishing houses expect their authors to actively market their books – often on their own dime.)

The advantage of the DIY model is that you own the copyright, and all proceeds go to you directly. You can still have your book listed on Amazon and other online retailers for a small fee, and your royalty payments are generally better than they would be through the traditional model.

The best way to make money with self-publishing is to buy copies of your book in bulk and sell them directly. Speak at conferences and rotary clubs. Get in front of people and tell them why your book matters. It helps if you are an entertaining speaker too. Audiences will buy your book because they want something tangible to take home as a reminder, kind of like purchasing merchandise after a concert.

The rise in eBook publishing also has revolutionized self-publishing. For little to no cost, I can release my novel on Amazon as an eBook for $2.99 and, with a lot of luck and some good marketing, make a tidy profit. Self-published titles are a steady presence on the *New York Times* and Amazon bestseller lists these days. Could this be the wave of the future? It's possible. But while eBook sales increased sharply for a number of years, they began to plateau in 2015.

I have no idea what the publishing industry will look like in ten years. But I do know this: if you want to write a novel, go for it. Do it for yourself. Do it for the people who matter most in your life. Whatever happens, at least you won't be one of those countless people who want to write a book but never have the work ethic or the courage to actually do it.

Acknowledgements

I am grateful to the staff and administration of Jordan High School, where I have worked for the past 14 years. Back in 2006, they encouraged me to develop a creative writing program and allowed me to teach multiple sections of it, even when this called for juggling on the part of our English department. I have taught some incredible students who have inspired me as a writer and as a teacher. This book would not exist without them. I am also eternally grateful to my beautiful wife, Jenni, and our two wonderful sons, Brett and Cason. I love the three of you with all of my heart.

About the Author

STUART ALBRIGHT is the recipient of the Milken National Educator Award (dubbed the "Oscars of Teaching" by *Teacher Magazine*.) In 2006, he was named the Durham Public Schools Teacher of the Year. Albright has a B.A. in English and Creative Writing from UNC Chapel Hill and an M.Ed. from Harvard University. He is the founder of McKinnon Press, a nonprofit that promotes literacy through the publishing of student work. He is also a freelance editor and lecturer on issues of urban education.

www.stuartalbright.com.

Made in the USA
Middletown, DE
08 October 2020

21410114R00073